MAGNETIC MINISTRY

INTENTIONALLY CREATING AN ATMOSPHERE THAT ATTRACTS

DANIEL L. LATIMER

CONTENTS

1

WHAT IS MINISTRY?

To properly evaluate the function and operation of ministry, it's going to be important that we have a clear understanding of what it means to be in ministry or to have a ministry. According to Merriam-Webster, ministry is the "service, function, or office of a minister of religion." From a spiritual standpoint, ministry is God's way of doing things.

1

Particularly, how we handle those who have been entrusted to us.

It's all about seeing and serving others from God's perspective. As we take a moment to examine the gospels, we'll find a very clear picture and pattern for how we should do both of those things. How we should see and serve. Jesus Christ, himself, encountered people from all walks of life. Some of them were weary travelers, sinners, beggars, the sick and infirmed or just people who were hungry for hope or some level of healing.

It's important to realize that Jesus did not just merely, haphazardly, observe their conditions, but he intentionally saw them. As we begin to discuss what ministry is, it's probably a good idea to begin to evaluate how you currently see people. From what vantage point do you determine who and what you currently serve?

For many people, their level of service is dependent on the amount of benefit they receive. Much of ministry will involve no material benefit or no substantial level of accolades to bring the spotlight to your front door. However, for those of us who are seeking a more purposeful life, those are the exact reasons why we do it. We don't engage in ministry to receive awards for what we do, but to receive an award from who we do it for. Why are you currently seeking a more expanded level of ministry? Who are you doing it for? Yourself or for God?

Jesus, in the illustration of the woman with the issue of blood, turns aside to see not only the condition of the person but also the purpose of the individual. This woman had a purpose that went beyond her issue. So often, we look at the issues of individuals and never think that not only does God want us to minister to them about their issue, but he also wants us to minister to them about their purpose.

I want you to realize something. Issues are bloody. They aren't beautiful and wonderful to look at sometimes. So, whenever we are ministering to anyone, it's probably a good idea to hear the heart of God about their purpose as well. Hearing God about their purpose will be the tool God will use to remove the shame and stir the honor of who he has created them to be.

The calling of ministry upon our lives should awaken another level of sight into the humanity and divinity of every individual that is touched by our message or our embrace.

Far too often, because of the hectic nature of our lives, seeing the authentic purpose of an individuals life is sometimes not even a thought. Ministry can become so fast-paced that we miss vital moments where God desires to use us the most. Often, there's not enough time to properly access the situation, or there's just too many people that require more than we have to offer at that given moment or time. If anything is to be said about how Jesus served, it would be that he was always one who took the time. We can see this clearly in the story of the woman with the issue of blood in the gospel according to Mark. She enters the scene as Jesus is in full ministry mode with Jairus. In a fit of desperation, she does what was uncommon in touching the garment of Jesus and bypassing the rules and regulations of that time that prohibited her from even being in the crowd. Jesus immediately feels that something miraculous has left him, turns around and asked a very powerful question, "Who touched me?". How awesome is that? He could've simply walked away and been a wonder among the people, but he took the time to recognize that not only was someone blessed through him but that someone had a need that he was qualified to meet.

As we engage in ministry, we must always keep to the forefront of our minds that there is something powerful hidden in us that God will only expose as we serve and minister to the needs of others.

It's a common misconception among the gifted and called, that our treasure is for us alone, meant to be used to build a legacy for ourselves. While in part, this is true, there's a greater message in the mission of our mantles. It's the idea that what's in and on me is meant to be used to cover someone else.

One of life's greatest callings is the calling to be a channel of support and care for someone else, literally, becoming a distribution center of a greater purpose forged through the commitment to a greater source. Sometimes this distribution will be in the spotlight as others watch on and gaze, but at other times working behind the scenes in the darkness of some of the most tragic of situations. It's at that time when no one's watching, where there's no one around to pat you on the back that your ministry is set apart for a greater role in God's redemptive plan towards man.

For many individuals, working behind the scenes is not glamorous enough or doesn't carry enough notoriety. In today's culture, many operate ministry from a prideful place to use others to make themselves look more powerful and prominent. However, true ministry is the giving of oneself for the benefit of someone else.

I, often, ask myself why do people serve at church or during some community agenda? For some individuals, it provides some feeling of being needed. For some, it's more of a sense of duty than it is anything else and then for some, they feel as though it is a God-given calling, and nothing makes them more satisfied. One of the things that I have learned is that life can make you so selfish. It can provide us with every reason possible to only do things that edify us personally while making others feels as though they don't add up or have enough of what's needed to be used of God and walk in purpose.

When we talk about seeing and serving people through the eyes of God, we must realize that God loves individuals far beyond what any of us can ever imagine. This pattern is the one that we are called to follow. It is the ability to love people beyond ourselves and to see our service to others as a greater mission in life than anything that could benefit ourselves.

One of the things that I fear is that many individuals will never realize that there is a difference between church and ministry. Church, at times, is a building where religious and traditional activities are performed. However, scripturally, the church in the Greek means ekklesia which is defined as "an assembly" or "called out ones." Therefore, the root meaning of the word church is not that of a building, but of people. Therefore, the essence of why we attend gatherings should be with an emphasis on building people and not things. It's interesting that when you ask people what church they attend, they usually automatically think of a building, but here's a better understanding of the idea of the church. It is the understanding that we are the church and we do ministry.

Our main duty as the church is to present hope and ultimately change lives. Our goal ultimately is to build people and not just build buildings. Our call is to supply the needs of people to better their lives and fulfill our own. How is your life fulfilled by serving others?

So often we make the mistake of assuming that doing church is doing ministry. Sadly, many individuals have been "doing" church for many years with little to no results of making a lasting impact on those around them. When I think of true ministry, I define it like this; it is the act of reaching outward to draw inward.

The act of reaching outwards means that even though it is an extension of yourself, it is not about yourself. It is about those that you have a passion for reaching and impacting. No, all of us aren't called to reach everyone. Some of us are called to reach a certain demographic, culture or area of life, but we are all called to touch someone.

To maximize our ministries, we must see people as Christ sees them. We can't see people as we see them if our view isn't pure, because that will be the nature in which we serve them. Perception is a vital component to ministry. It is hard to help people you don't genuinely love. Throughout scripture it is stated that many times before Jesus healed or performed a miracle for anyone, He was moved with compassion first. It was His heart of love that fueled His ministry. You can't love ministry while hating people.

The foundation of everything we do for God must be love. It bothers me when I see people preach the gospel with so much anger and madness. It's hard to believe that anyone could think that this would draw anyone to Christ. Anger and fear are never the tools that Christ uses to draw people to the Father.

Jeremiah 31:3, states it like this, "The Lord hath appeared of old unto me, saying, Yea, I have loved thee with an everlasting love. Therefore, with loving-kindness have I drawn thee."

More than praying for what to say, we must begin to pray that we speak from a pure heart. So many have been driven away from God because of the lack of love we express. If we looked closely at the development of the disciples in scripture, we would find that they too didn't always demonstrate the heart of God. So, it was a learning process for them, as it is for us as well.

On one notable occasion, they told Jesus to send the crowds away. What this displayed was a lack of compassion. It's easy to enjoy having Christ as a part of your life without actually having the love of Christ in your heart. There was another instance, where a man was trying to get the help of Jesus for his daughter, and other individuals came and asked him, "Why, troublest the master any further." Sometimes insensitivity in all aspects of life has driven people away from the help they need. They felt as though his cry for help was an inconvenience. It messed up their agenda. Let me ask you something. What's the true agenda you have towards ministry? It's easy to go into ministry with the idea that you want to help people, but then the idea of fame begins to block why you originally signed up. It's a great idea to go back and revisit your beginning plans and goals, evaluate how and if you've achieved them and if you haven't, create ways to do that and more.

Here's another example of how insensitivity can push others away. Do you remember the time when Mary was worshipping Jesus and poured expensive fragrance on his feet, and Judas was so concerned about the price of the ointment that he missed the true essence of worship? Could it be that many can't effectively do ministry because they see people through the lens of commodity and currency but not with compassion and concern?

I desire that as you read this book, that you will be overwhelmed with a true desire to see and serve as Jesus did, this is the heart of God.

2

THE CONTENT AND CONTEXT OF MINISTRY

Before anyone decides to work in any area of ministry, he or she needs to understand two vital elements. One is the context of ministry and the other being the content of ministry.

Context is the circumstances that form the setting for an event, statement, or idea. Content is things that are held and included in something.

THE CONTEXT OF MINISTRY

The context of ministry will always be PEOPLE. These people include those who have already come to Christ, those who will come to Christ, those who have come to Christ and gone astray, and those who will never come to Christ.

Ministry is primarily about people. Doesn't that sound like stating the obvious? Well, actions speak louder than words. By watching some leaders, you could get the impression that being in ministry is about all sorts of things. It's sometimes hard to recognize the real focus behind what we do as leaders sometimes.

Some people act as though local church ministry is primarily about maintenance. These type of people will give everything they have for ministry, but only with the intent of maintaining what has been built, instead of investing in what hasn't been seen yet. I'm speaking of people. Countless people are simply waiting on an atmosphere to be created that will not only attract them but also develop them.

I heard one lady's response when threatened with the closure of a church speak in defiance, saying, "I swore to my father that as long as I live on this earth, the doors of this church would never close." Her defiance was not out of a heart to reach others, but more from a desire to maintain what was. Many people fear the evolution of church ministry and will do everything in their power to keep things just the way it is. Even if this means hindering others from being a part of it.

There is nothing wrong wanting to maintain ministry, but let's not forget the mission behind our efforts.

Many churches have no plans for outreach; it just wants to maintain itself. Why? Certainly not for those outside its walls. They have lost sight of the idea that the church should exist primarily for those who are not its members. God is concerned about people. He's not concerned about denominations, race, creed, but all of humanity. If you only focus on ministering to people within your organization or denomination, then you have missed God's heart concerning ministry and His people. Humanity is the only reason God sent his son Jesus. The angels couldn't even fathom God's view of people until they asked: "What is man that thou are so mindful of them?" In other words, they were interested in this creation that had caught God's heart and focus. The full essence of the heart of God is love, and that love is towards the people that he has created for his glory.

Our ministries should be diverse because Christians are composed of all types of individuals. No one should feel blocked from coming to our churches. Therefore, we must intentionally create structures that "draw all men" to him, this takes work and intentional effort.

Also, ministry is a lifestyle devoted to making much of Christ and meeting the needs of others. It means that we "do good to everyone, especially to those who are of the household of faith" according to Galatians 6:10. Regardless, of the fact that we might be bankers or educators, athletes or artists, it means that we aim at advancing other people's faith for the glory of God. It's all about people.

Ministry is not self-centered. It's not about us. You must completely forget about yourself and desires to become productive and serve others. Once again, it's not about you.

Here's something to always keep at the forefront of your mind. God only uses us as conduits to flow through so that He can reach His people.

So, no matter what title you have or what gift you possess, you have received it to serve people. One day the disciples asked Jesus, "Who will be the greatest in the Kingdom?" In turn, Jesus took a towel and started washing their feet, replying, "Let the greatest among you, be the servant." They were concerned about a TITLE, but God gave them a TOWEL. Kingdom success is in Kingdom service. Even in business, true wealth is often discovered while serving people. People are God's Passion.

THE CONTENT OF MINISTRY

The Content of ministry is the Gospel, which is the death, burial, and resurrection of Jesus Christ. The fact that God sent His only begotten son, Jesus, as a ransom for our sins that we might be redeemed. It was his death that has become our life. We must never stray away from the Gospel message.

The gospel is God's method for bringing us to himself. The true source of our salvation, help, deliverance, security, and hope. It is not only the announcement of a better way to live but also the channel that we enter God's Kingdom. But this isn't sometimes a quick thing - it is a lifelong educational process. The gospel is God's system of impressing upon us a certain destination and how we should live so that we will reach it. His message of "good news" has tremendous power to motivate us and propel us in the right direction. The only thing we must do is truly believe.

God demonstrates his ability towards humanity in a variety of ways. Sometimes the gospel of Jesus Christ is like a hammer wielded in the hands of a man, breaking the stony heart that is without his love. There are also occasions where the gospel is like a consuming fire that ignites in the places of our hearts that are the coldest and then at other times; it's like a mother or fathers embrace, comforting us in ways that only a loving parent can.

We cannot disconnect our ministries from the preaching of the gospel and cut people off from the channel that will give them their greatest of victories and triumphs.

Churches who preach the gospel are those who are filled with individuals that really get it. They understand fully how much the gospel has helped them and how much they desire for it to help others as well. These individuals know that Jesus came for real sinners who have a real need for real power from a powerfully risen Savior.

Many things may change, but the message of the gospel must be concrete and rock solid. We must never corrupt the Gospel to be popular. Many have done it in the name of being contemporary or universal. Some of them have done it with great intentions, but with terrible results.

Our culture has adapted so many doctrines and belief systems that have compromised our convictions and ultimately driven us away from our foundation. Jesus Christ is still the only way. There is no other name given unto man whereby men can be saved but by the name of Jesus. This understanding is the essence of the Gospel, and we must refuse to contaminate its content.

It's important that we don't lose the purity of the gospel of Jesus Christ, what we live for and who we worship. In today's trends and cultures, it's sometimes easier said than done. Satan is a master counterfeit and will provide many things that look like the gospel but are not. If we are easily manipulated, because of the popularity of another individual, we can fall into it without noticing. Whatever is not the full gospel is a lie and will ultimately lead to the death of our purpose and passion in Christ Jesus.

Our souls must be fed with the gospel, if not, then they will be fed the food of the idols of this world. Social media, sports, entertainment, self-satisfaction, relationships, business and many more things can become the idols that take us away from the reality of the mission of the gospel.

Here's what the pure gospel teaches us. It teaches us that we couldn't and can never save ourselves. It is only through the complete work of Christ that any of us can truly embrace all that he came to bring.

As we engage in the call of ministry, it is vital that we stay within the confines of biblical standards. We may not keep a rock method, but we must have a rock message. As believers we must avoid being CARNAL in our worship, we must not compromise our witness, and more importantly, we must refuse to corrupt the Word.

So, in a nutshell, ministry is about service and to effectively do that, one must have a clear understanding of context and content. Who the message is for and what the message truly is. Only then will we be able to know what true ministry is.

3

THE POWER TO DRAW

Have you ever wondered why people are attracted to you? It's not like you're doing anything spectacular, but they love being around you. They also feel the need to confide in you and ask you for counsel concerning things that they would never dare to share with anyone else. The reason for this is because God has placed a magnetic anointing on your life. A magnet is as a person or thing that can attract. It's call influence. It's the ability to draw people in your direction. All of us have that unique thing about us that attracts people. Whether it's singing, public speaking, writing, athleticism, music, law, medicine, designing, etc. Whatever God has given you to draw people is for His glory.

There are many types of magnets, but there are two I want to discuss briefly. First, let's start by talking about permanent magnets. Permanent magnets are those we are most familiar with, such as the magnets hanging on our refrigerators doors. They are permanent in the sense that once they are magnetized, they retain a level of magnetism. Secondly, there are temporary magnets. These types of magnets are those who act like a permanent magnet when they are within a strong magnetic field but lose their magnetism when the magnetic field disappears. Examples would be like paperclips and nails and other soft iron items.

God wants us to be permanent magnets for him. We should be able to retain our level of spiritual magnetism. Unfortunately, many have become temporary magnets who start off drawing, but through the process of time, they lose their ability to draw. We will go deeper into this topic in a few chapters.

God expects us to use our gifts to draw people to Christ. It could be your smile, personality, or a sense of humor that attracts people. Whatever it is, use it for the benefit of bettering people. I think sometimes we underestimate the impact we can make in the lives of others. Sometimes we look at it as us just being ourselves and fail to realize how many people we come in contact every day that are eternally affected by being in our presence.

When I was younger in school, I was the class clown. Everyone liked being around me because I was fun and full of laughs. Even now I have my super silly side. But I remember my mother telling me after coming from meetings with my teacher because I had gotten in trouble disrupting the class, she would say, "Daniel, you can lead people the right way or the wrong way. You can lead them to hell or heaven". She was saying that I had influence, but I was using it the wrong way. In a spiritual sense, you must ask yourself how are you using your ability to draw?

The closer we are personally and physically to others, the greater our influence is over them, and the greater their influence is in our lives as well. Even more interestingly, unlike our attempts to control, our attempts to influence don't require our conscious intent, therefore our ability to influence others is so much more important than our ability to control them. We're always exerting influence simply by being who we are, saying what we say, and doing what we do, the only real choice we have in the matter is whether the influence we exert is for God's glory or our gain.

Ultimately, Jesus is the real magnet. The message of the cross is the power to draw. John 12:32 says, "If I am lifted up from the earth, I will draw all people to Myself." In our church culture, we have misinterpreted that passage. The phrase "lifted up" here has nothing to do with praise. Lifted points back to the lifting of the serpent in the wilderness (John 3:14-16). When Jesus said, "If I be lifted…" He was referring to His death on the cross.

It is the death of Christ that has given us victory, not praise. Praise is good, and praise is necessary, but praise is not what gives us the ultimate victory. The crucifixion of Jesus is our victory.

When Jesus died, He broke the enemy's hold on us. He removed the chains that enslaved us. He broke the power of death, hell, and the grave.

Paul in Galatians 6:14 is saying, "I have nothing to offer you but Jesus." He is the ultimate drawing tool. If we offer Jesus without contamination or our dogma, we will be able to draw souls continually. **JESUS IS ENOUGH!** Our job as believers is to get to know Christ and then make Him known.

In a culture that's developing new concepts, beliefs, and doctrines, it's becoming more of a challenge to draw souls. Our drawing method must be strategic and spiritual. We must seek God as to how to reach this culture. The bible states, "the god of this world have blinded the minds of the people that they may not believe" so our approach must not appeal to the emotions of the people but more so the mind and spirit.

Proverbs 11:30 states, "he that winneth souls is wise." Two words in this passage are worth considering and are quite noteworthy. First, the word is "win" which would imply that there is a competition or opposition. We are fighting against something or someone and must have a plan so that we can win. It denotes the fact that there is a battle. Secondly, there's that word "soul." Our job is to win the soul. The fight is for the soul of the individual. Now to appreciate this text, we must properly define the word soul so that we can stand within the line of context.

Soul in the Greek is the word "psyche" (to breathe) the mental abilities of a living being: reason, character, feeling, consciousness, memory, perception, thinking, etc. So, when the writer says he that winneth a soul is wise, he is saying that our responsibility is to talk to the end in which we capture the mind and convince the intellect. Our message must be not only spiritual but also psychological. This is a generation and culture of thinkers. Therefore, you can't reach them through feelings alone. We must study and be accurate as it relates to information we will share, and we must be able to articulate with precision and persuasion.

Systems are in place in the world to capture the soul. Even in the simplest form. Television commercials and advertisements are strategic in how they present product and the likes. They do it in a way that stimulates the mind which in turn spark desire. If you watch television for long enough in one day, you will see certain commercials multiple times throughout the day. The purpose is to repeatedly capture your attention with the same thing until you can't resist.

Have you ever gone to a car dealership or store without the intent to purchase anything and only to look but the salesmen talks to you with such a convincing tone until you finally give in? You may even say no in the beginning, but they keep giving you details that become more and more interesting throughout the dialogue. Suddenly you find yourself in an office signing the papers or at the register purchasing the item. What that salesman has successfully done is captured your soul. That same principle applies to the Kingdom of God in the topic of drawing souls. Let's be clear; we are not to antagonize, aggravate or nag. That type of behavior drives instead of draws. Our mandate is to be compassionate, consistent, but also patient.

We are not luring people but drawing them. To lure gives the connotation of deception and manipulation. We will use the truth as our magnet. We don't have to con or trick people to get them to follow us. These things have been done in the body of Christ in the name of ministry. It's important to understand that gimmicks and games are not needed. The only time you see gimmicks in ministry is when people are trying to draw others to themselves. Pride becomes the motivation. Gimmicks are birthed from greed. Those who are hungry for attention and currency. They need the applause of men to feel better about themselves. So, they use the power and gift to draw adoration to themselves instead of God. But when the objective is to draw and lead people to Christ, purity and truth become the root. You cannot lead anyone to Christ through impure avenues. The way must be pure and truthful and more importantly, the only person that is to get glory and credit, is God.

Whenever glory and honor are more important to us than God, it becomes idolatry. Sure, God will allow us to receive compliments and accolades as forms of rewards for serving Him, but that's not the objective. It must always be clear that we are servants and God is Sovereign.

Pray today that God will cause you to maximize your sphere of influence and that you will walk boldly in your gifts and talents so that you can effectively draw for the glory of God. Don't be timid or afraid. Be confident that when you open your mouth, someone will be attracted to your voice. When you smile, someone will be affected in a good way, when you work your gifts and calling someone will be forever impacted. Even when you're not saying or doing anything, ask God to make your presence alone effective and captivating to the degree that people want to talk to you and get to know you. When that happens, that will be your opportunity to plant seeds that will ultimately lead to Jesus Christ.

4

REACHING THE UNREACHED

It is so easy to lose sight of our original assignment by getting distracted by the culture. The church in and of itself has two major assignments. One is to gather, and the other is to scatter. We gather for power, but we scatter to proclaim. The greatness of a church is not measured by how many people come into the church but in how many go out in ministry.

One of Jesus's main goals while on the earth was to develop a strategy for his disciples to reach those far away from him. He outlines this goal by instructing them in Matthew 28:19. He clearly instructs them to "Go and make disciples of all nations." The operative word here is "go." There's a demand placed upon the life of every believer to commit to distribute the gospel. Simply said, Jesus was communicating in Matthew 28:19, the importance of establishing a community that wasn't afraid to witness and that wasn't afraid of their witness.

Let's take a moment to discuss a few reasons why people may be afraid to display their witness. It can be because of a certain environment of their neighborhood, business, social circle or even their family. Sometimes we are placed in environments that are not comfortable for our belief systems to be displayed. But it is in those exact environments where our witness has the greatest ability to thrive and flourish. The believers need to be bold can never be underestimated.

The boldness that I'm speaking of is not about a certain aspect of our personality. This type of boldness is the action of the Holy Spirit within us that is the result of a conviction much stronger than anyone can believe. If you don't possess a conviction about the gospel, you won't have the necessary courage to face opposition or the ability to stand in the midst of threats or defiance. Individuals who are fearful are rarely those who will exert the necessary boldness to share the gospel with those who are far away from him.

We must understand that it is not the Lord's desire that anyone perishes, but that all have the opportunity to come to him. But this is often hindered because of the lack of skilled laborers who boldly go into the field. It's easy to share the gospel with those that know it, but for many, they find it a cumbersome task to share the gospel with those who may not be familiar with church or with God at all.

The church must go outside of its walls to reach people who need the Lord. The effectiveness of our churches depends on the number of people who are involved in meaningful ministry.

Ministry starts when the church sends people to go out into the community to share the good news of Jesus in practical ways. Ministry cannot happen when people do not serve. We have been redeemed for a reason, converted for a cause, and saved for service.

You cannot be saved by performing service or ministry, that comes only through Jesus Christ, "for by grace are ye saved through faith; and that not of yourselves: it is the gift of God. Not of works lest any man should boast." However, the world, as well as those in the church, see our faith by our works or service. Now I want to set before you a theory: if God is to be glorified by our life of service/ministry, it is safe to assume that everyone in the church should be involved in service/ministry. God has set the church in place to minister to the world around her and has sovereignly placed members in the body for ministry.

God ordained the church for the world. So, if we never go into the world, then we defeat the purpose of the church. 2 Corinthians 4:3 states, "if our gospel is hidden, it's hidden to them that are lost." In many cases, we preach the gospel to people who already know Christ or have at least been introduced to Him. We spend time, saving saved people. But there is a whole world filled with those who have never heard the gospel preached, never been to church or who don't have a church background. There are people who we pass on the way to church who we have never offered even a kind word.

How often do we pass up opportunities to be a witness? It is easy to get distracted from the call while doing religious activities.

Why do we preach the gospel? We preach Jesus because of the bondage and blindness inherit to the world. Our goal is to bring insight and enlightenment but also to set the captives free. I've been in ministry since I was fourteen years old. I have counseled and been a life coach to many, and one thing that I know for sure is many people are in bondage, and they want to be free, but they don't know how.

I have witnessed sinners crying out for help because they didn't want to be the way they were, but demonic spirits had such a stronghold on them. These individuals needed someone who had a pure anointing to break the grip of satanic power off their lives. Some have been living with habits and addictions for so long that they have become accustomed to their lifestyle until they don't even see themselves living free. Often they die in their lifestyles because no one has the patience or the compassion to help. Everyone is focused on their success and ambitions until the lost isn't even a concern. We have developed an attitude that says, "every man for himself" when the truth is God never called us for us. He chose us for others. Every gift and anointing is for someone else, and we become displeasing to God when we are selfish and arrogant as if we're someone special.

One of the most heartfelt things that we can ask God to have is a soft heart towards sinners. If you are a leader but your community doesn't know it, then you're not an effective leader. Your community no matter how big or small should know you're there and ready to be a support to them even when they might not currently be a part of your congregation. It's all about building the Body of Christ, not just your church. Of course, everyone won't know you, but there should be a track record of your involvement with the homeless, the hungry, and the hurting. There should be something that identifies your church with the community.

Many are waiting for sinners to come to them when the Great Commission in scripture instructs us to go to them. There are two key essentials that God has admonished every believer to be to reach the unreached. First, we are to be **LIGHT.** The bible says, "Let your light so shine amongst men so they will see your good works and glorify your father in heaven." We are light in a dark world. Why are moths drawn to light? Moths use the moon to navigate in the darkness, so they are only doing what comes naturally to them, but unconverted people prefer the darkness and don't like the light because it exposes sin.

Jesus said, "I am the light of the world. Whoever follows me will not walk in darkness but will have the light of life" (John 8:12) and then tells us in

Matthew 5:14, "ye are the light of the world. A city set on a hill that cannot be hidden". What He is saying is that if you truly have the Light of the world living in you, it can't be hidden. Others are drawn to that light like a moth to a porchlight, so when they come to you, point them to the Light of the world.

Secondly, we are to be **SALT.** Jesus said, "You are the salt of the earth, but if salt has lost its taste, how shall its saltiness be restored? It is no longer good for anything except to be thrown out and trampled under people's feet" (Matt 5:13). Salt that's lost its taste doesn't help enhance the taste of food but makes it bitter. It's good for nothing except, as Romans did, using it as part of the Roman Road system the built, so then it would be trampled under people's feet. Our prayer should be "Lord don't allow me to become a **SALTLESS SAINT.**" Even with being the salt of the earth we must have balance. Too much salt turns it bitter, and too little salt makes things bland, so we need to have just the right amount to enhance people's lives.

5

MAINTAINING PROPER MOTIVES

What do you think matters the most to God, the way we do things or the reason we do them? Sometimes, we can become so infatuated with performing a service that we lose sight of why we are doing them. This loss of sight opens the door to the wrong energy placed behind it and the wrong expectation of reward. When you are doing ministry for God, and with that in mind it's often difficult to expect too much from people. I'm not saying that there won't be times when God will use someone to bless you because of what you have done, but that's not your primary expectation. Your primary expectation is that God will reward you and your main hope is that he will be pleased with your service.

Believe it or not, people can tell when you are doing something for personal gain or making a name for yourself. One of the greatest lessons the life of Jesus taught us, was that he "made of himself no reputation." It wasn't important that he had a famous name if the life he lived made his name great. There's a complete difference in seeking the fame and the Lord making your name great because of your humility and proper motives.

I'm sure that many of us can recall instances where we have heard of a leader who made ministry all about themselves. Sadly, for some of these leaders, their sense of importance collided with the mission they were called to achieve. But it's most likely that these very individuals entered ministry honestly wanting to serve others, not attempting to build this great dynasty. But somewhere on the journey, they got a taste of fame or glory and that one sweet moment increased into something that would get wildly out of control.

One of the greatest ways to avoid vainglory is to stay in the presence of God. Whenever we submit to God in prayer, it is very hard to get us to be submitted to anything else, even ourselves. The presence of God is what fuels our passions, and it's also what keeps us from perverting a pure mission in ministry. How many leaders do you hear boasting on their submission to prayer? You can probably count on one hand how many of your colleagues share with you about praying and spending time with the Lord. But here's the other side of the coin. You don't spend time with God solely for getting a message that will make you look even greater than you think you are. You spend time with God to deal with yourself, to ensure that your heart remains pure and the God always remain the focal point of your ministry and life. Christ must remain your goal amidst the roaring cheers of those who love your ministry.

Another destructive element to maintaining proper motives in ministry is your rejection of other credible sources of counsel. So many times, we see true leaders destroyed by self-ambition because of their failure to acknowledge their ignorance in certain areas.

As much as we would like people to believe, we do not know everything, and sometimes our way is not the best way a situation can be handled.

You must enter into ministry realizing that along the way you will need wise counsel. You'll always need individuals who have the wisdom of God, and you'll have to trust that what they are saying is the truth. It's easy to ask for counsel, but sometimes it's very hard to listen. Listening to the advice of others takes humility, and for many leaders, pride will cause them to know it's the best route, but force them to take what they know isn't going to work.

Here's what the Bible says about wise counsel in Proverbs 11:14: "Where there is no guidance, a people fall, but in an abundance of counselors there is safety."

It's also important to note that even when seeking counsel, you must ensure that it is Godly counsel. Sometimes we make the worst of decisions because the person we consulted didn't have a heart for God and certainly not a heart for the ministry we lead. Make sure that you're going to a person that is referencing your situation from a God view and not a view of their past mistakes and feelings about a situation. Also, ensure that the individual has a proven track record in prayer as well. Individuals that have a solid prayer life are more sensitive to the voice of God and the direction that you might need to take.

As we continue to talk about maintaining proper motives, I want to take some time discussing the importance of remaining humble. Ministry affords us the opportunity to speak many right things at the right time to people that need it. With this, sometimes comes great appreciation and remaining humble is a place that you'll have to fight to remain.

Just think about it. You don't have to fight humility when you are wrong. It comes naturally to most rational people. But you do have to fight it when you're right. Pride comes quickly, and you'll have to recognize it for what it is if you're going to keep your motives pure.

We exist in a culture that will do anything to promote, exalt, progress or place the spotlight on themselves, even at the expense of helping others. So, we are called to exhibit the exact opposite. We have to display a life that is selfless, but prosperous and a life that is humble, without being weak.

Pride is a very dangerous enemy. Especially, to those of us who are called to serve others and who can influence others. Countless scriptures speak about pride, and none of them are as clear to us as the illustration of Lucifers fall in heaven. He was gifted but doomed because of the pride that arose in his heart against the Father.

Have you ever thought of being prideful as a direct opposition against God? If we think about it whenever we are prideful, we are more about ourselves then we are about the source of our abundance. Nebuchadnezzar found himself in this position. He looked over his vast empire and proclaimed how great he was to had built it. His pride displeased God, and in response, the mind of Nebuchadnezzar was thrown into a fog leading his unfortunate wilderness experience. His experience in the wilderness was ended when he came to himself by recognizing that it was God who had given him the strength, ability and might to build what he did. The illustrations we just spoke of are extreme instances, but the moral of the stories are so clear. Don't allow unfortunate situations to be the cause of your humility. Be humble now, so that you won't have to be humbled later.

Being a person of humility doesn't mean that you are without confidence or strength, but it does mean that your motives are always placed at the submission to the one you serve.

One of the greatest ways that you can also maintain pure motives is by remembering that your greatness is attached to your service. Jesus states this general principle of greatness in Mark 9:35, "Sitting down, he called the twelve and said to them, 'If anyone wants to be first, he shall be last of all and servant of all.'" How many of us view greatness like this? For most people, greatness is the size of their sanctuary, the number of their members or the number of achievements they've accomplished. But that's not how Jesus views it. He views the measure of our greatness in the level of our submission to service.

The concept of greatness is a discussion we often have with ourselves and others. Sometimes it's an open discussion, but at other times it's just about how we view one another. During sporting events, we attempt to determine who's going to win the activity by sizing up the players, recounting their track records and statistics. This is also how we behave when evaluating our self-image and the image of those around us. We want to know that in comparison to others that we are as great as they are, and sometimes we hope that we are greater.

In Luke 9:46, the disciples begin what would be an interesting discussion. They had been with the Lord for a few years and thought that they were special men. Pause, let's stop there for a moment. We're not special in the sense of being above everyone else. We are special because of the special assignment we have as believers. Watch how important you become in your own eyes because the spirit of entitlement will cause you to believe that you deserve things that you don't.

The disciples at this time begin to argue among themselves regarding who the greatest would be. At this time, the disciples were just like the crowds of people they often ignored. Each of them, no doubt, was sizing up the other. Peter was probably among them talking about him walking on water, having the keys and being the one who boldly declared that Jesus was the one who had the words of eternal life. So, as we can see it's very easy to feel entitled to greatest when you are viewing greatness through the lens of what you have done in life or for God.

It's important that you don't allow your perception of greatness to be dependent on the particular place you're seated. In life and ministry, your seats will change. In the area that you are popular in today, might not be the area that you are popular in tomorrow and if you are basing your greatness on what's popular, you'll leave purpose often in search for it.

WHAT'S THE MOTIVE OF YOUR CHURCH?

The motive of the church can be seen in the current structure of your church. A church without an evangelism mission isn't structured for sinners and souls. Christ established the church with a great commission and the absence of this displays motives that are outside of our original commandment. Many leaders have structured the houses they lead for church service, but not for ministry

Here are a few reasons why we don't evangelize:

1. **Lack of passion for the lost:** We love to worship but hate witness. We'll enjoy the experience of the gathering, but don't share the experience with others outside. We love the security of the sanctuary.

2. **We are not fully converted:** When we are converted, we are fully changed ourselves. We should be disturbed when we see people lost and hurting. As we see in the gospels, the disciples had a habit in their immaturity of desiring that the lost be sent away. They displayed at times, given their

own needs and desires, a lack of love and mercy. This is an example of the hard-hearted believer.

3. **We fail to understand the purpose of the church:** We structure our church according to our perception. Structuring your ministry based on your view of things can be dangerous. We must build as unto the Lord, and this includes building according to the way the church was established.

4. **Fear of being rejected:** You can't soul win when you fear being rejected. Many individuals don't share the gospel with others, because they fear the sting that rejection gives. They need to be welcomed and invited, but sometimes that's not going to happen. Your sharing of the gospel must be out of a heart that truly

wants to share his love and word with others. Also, many don't share with others because they lack confidence in what they are saying.

5. **Lives are bad examples:** Simply said, it's hard to share about Christ when your life doesn't line. Let your life line-up with your lips.

6

CREATING A SAFE HAVEN

It would amaze you how many people are overwhelmed by living in such a fallen culture. It seems like sometimes more people that we can imagine are crushed by the sinful burden of their present, past, and sometimes they are without hope for the future. This burden affects everything they touch, their relationships and even their ministries. What's sadder is that many people don't feel as though they can come to church and be protected even in the midst of their issues. The church has become unsafe for the sinner.

Self-righteousness is an evil beast. You would think that those of us who have been such recipients of his grace would be compelled to display it towards others, but that doesn't happen in most cases. In most cases, we look at the sinner with some level of disdain. Like, "Why can't they stop?" or "Why can't they get themselves together?". I, sometimes think, that many of us who are in leadership should at certain intervals go on a memory vacation. Start thinking about all of the crazy things that you have done, how God intervened, restored and made you the example that you are today. It is not only a humbling experience, but it would also be a sobering one.

Sometimes people are living in quiet desperation. They are desperate for love, support, light and many times, life itself. It can never be underestimated the effects that sin has on the soul, spirit, and body.

Friends, if there should be one place where individuals could come and find support, patience, and compassion it should be the church. However, the church hasn't been as safe as one would suppose.

So, many people have resorted to running to phone apps, illicit relationships, the darkness of night in their situation, attempting to find some relief to the demons they face. Would God be pleased if this is what sinners are saying about our churches? I think the answer is clear, No.

One of the reasons why individuals aren't comfortable in our churches is that it's not a safe place to confess. Confession is a biblical instruction, but can often lead to a person being shunned, disgraced, mocked and even pushed out of our churches by those who deem themselves more righteous. What have you done to ensure that your ministry is a safe place where individuals can come, share their faults and then receive the ministry and support for them to overcome victoriously?

Here's what the church is not. The church is not like the gym. It's not the place where people come to improve their bodies. The church is a hospital where the death of sin is made no more through the power of the resurrection, that is Jesus Christ. We have created a social club, instead of training physicians who are led by the great physician. The church is the place where those who have been beaten, bruised, scarred and destitute should be able to come and find recovery and healing for whatever is ailing them.

But instead, we have become more damaging to the sinner that we can see needs healing.

JUST TALK ABOUT IT!

Sometimes, individuals who are struggling with certain vices feel as though they are the only one that is dealing with it. Often, they feel as though no one else understands and that the gospel can't touch that part of their lives. One of the greatest ways the church can connect the dots is by talking about it all.

Don't simply point out the popular sins of our day without including the ones that might be a little risky. How many times have you gotten tired of hearing messages about promiscuity? Not because it's not the truth, but because you know that they are so many others that individuals are experiencing and not getting deliverance from. Sadly, many sinners will leave the church because they feel disconnected where deliverance is regarded. They see the altar calls for the smokers, for the promiscuous, for the adulterers, but they don't see any for those who are on the brink of suicide, for those who are cutting themselves or who have dark desires to hurt others. There are people right now in your ministry who deal with these things, and if you don't help them see the glorious light and hope of the gospel, they'll be overwhelmed with the burden, and it might result in further damage to their life and purpose.

JESUS SAT WITH SINNERS

One of the other reasons that sinners don't feel comfortable in our churches is that they don't hear anyone else speaking about their issues. It's extremely hard to open up about things that are so dark when everyone else acts as though they can't relate. Sometimes, it's a good idea, even if it's in small settings to be transparent about your history. Guess what? We all have a history, and for many believers, it's not too far gone. This has to be done in a way that is transparent without becoming a stumbling block to someone else. The intention behind any level of sharing is to guide the hearers into the hope that has delivered you. Your church needs to know that the person that is speaking to them knows very well how easy it is to get stuck while showing them the power of the gospel that gave you light in your dark situations

When we see Jesus talking to the woman at the well, we see that she was defensive at first, but through the wisdom and patience Jesus exhibited towards her, she was able to lower her guard and receive what she needed. He took time with her. This is one of the missing elements in our ministries. It's the power of patience. Often, people won't be transformed overnight. Most of us weren't. Total transformation in most instances takes time, and we must be willing to know the darkest of things about people, support them spiritually and give them time to digest the light that will ultimately bring them out fully.

When a person has been bound for years, their deliverance is not usually received overnight.

Jesus offered the woman at the well hope. Even though, he knew her issues. He discussed them with her without judgment and offered her a better solution which was himself. In return, she goes and brings many more people to him to receive the same thing that she just had.

Your ministry should be designed to offer the same solution this woman received and should be resulting in others just like them being drawn to your church because it is safe.

Here are a few ways that Jesus made sinners feel safe with him:

- Jesus was an approachable leader
- Jesus expressed love in everything he said
- Jesus was sensitive to what others needed
- Jesus was a part of the lives of others

Jesus's demonstration of this type of leader helped those who were following learn how to express love through the Holy Spirit to everyone they encountered.

WHAT DOES YOUR LOVE LOOK LIKE?

If we compare Jesus and the way he loved with the way most of us love today, we would probably not like the comparison we saw. Jesus was the perfect example of compassion. Whenever there was a need, he was always willing to meet it, especially, when it came to coming to the defense of others. Do you remember the story of the woman who was caught in adultery? Though many people were ready to stone and judge her, he defended her. He stepped in and silenced the vicious crowd, gave her instructions of hope and sent her on her way. He refused to condemn what he came on earth to redeem.

When we speak about creating a haven, we are talking about the total atmosphere of your ministry. When we speak of support, we are not talking about upholding wrong or sin, but more about how to develop an atmosphere that supports the individual as they are walking through their process of deliverance. You can attempt to get the person delivered and as a result, end up damaging or destroying them in the process.

In the Bible, we understand that it was not legal for a person who had leprosy to be in the crowd or around healthy individuals. They had to shout their condition so that others would be aware of them. They were isolated to only being with people just like them. Doesn't this sound like some of our ministries? We don't like associating, because we feel as though people will think we are just like them or we are afraid that what's on them will somehow jump on us? This kind of thinking is absurd.

The power of the gospel compels us not to shun the sinner or those who are walking through dark places. It teaches us that God can reach down to the lowest valley to pull anyone out and will leave the ninety-nine, to get that one. This behavior should be the heart of our ministries because this is the heart of God.

7

PROTECTING THE MAGNET

There's an undeniable treasure on the inside of you that draws people to you. It's most likely very noticeable to everyone around you. It's powerful and in many instances rare among your colleagues, family, and friends. You're a gift.

With every gift, comes an awesome responsibility. This responsibility is to not only value what you have been given, but to protect it so that it lasts. For many people, this is one of the hardest of tasks. This task is to be very conscious of things and or people that might devalue it and sometimes destroy it.

The truth of the matter is that there will always be people that we like or even love that will not be as vigilant about protecting you or your gift as you will be. They'll not see the danger in certain things and might even encourage you to gamble with losing it or its effectiveness in your purpose. The idea here is that the main responsibility on protecting the thing that God is using in your life is up to you and no one else.

A lot of times, we roll over this responsibility on to our intercessors, friends, leaders, and congregations. We want them to watch out for us at all times, but as with humans, sometimes they either forget or get to caught up in their own lives. So, it's us that have to know what we have, value it above anything else and do whatever we have to do to ensure that it stays operable.

In scripture, Samson was given a wonderful gift, that was introduced to his parents with detailed instructions. They were told what he could do and what he couldn't for his strength to stay viable and the deliverance of many to remain progressive. Think about this. God places this responsibility on Samson, because not only did he want to bless Samson's parents with a child, he also wanted to bless Israel with deliverance from the Philistines. See, your gift is not only designed to be an honor to you but also the freedom to others.

As the story of Samson unfolds, we discover that Samson is not as serious about safeguarding his strength. Sometimes, we can become so comfortable being used that we take lightly the accountability needed to maintain it. We become common with an uncommon anointing.

Samson doesn't lose it all at once. It is a progressive dismantling of his ability to withstand the persistence of the enemy. As you look at your life and ministry, I want you to look at the areas that have been persistent thorns and areas of weakness. Sometimes it's not that it's this major thing right now but can become one in the future. Therefore, we must become bold whenever we encounter things and people that go against what we know is not right. Remember this, what is good for one might not be good for all.

There are some restrictions that God places on you, that he might not place on another leader. The magnet within you is particular to your ministry, life, purpose, and journey and attempting to follow the same guidelines as a brother or sister is dangerous.

As you may have read, Samson falls terribly and loses what God used so mightily. He is blinded and imprisoned because of his failure to protect what God had given him. The joy of the story is that Samson recovers, but he doesn't live beyond it. His hair grows back, but his sight is lost. He kills more Philistines in his death than in his life, but he doesn't survive to enjoy the victory. Sometimes, our recovery and restoration don't include us getting back the thing that was drawn to us. Some things are forever lost because of our inability to protect the magnet.

GUARDING YOUR MIND

One of the greatest ways to protect the magnet is to protect your mind. What you place in front of your eyes, allow to enter your ears, and the audience you keep has a lot to do with how protected you remain. When I speak of being protected, I am not referring to being guarded. I'm speaking about how to be conscious of what you are carrying.

Here's what 1 Peter 5:8 says, "Be alert and of sober mind. Your enemy, the devil, prowls around like a roaring lion looking for someone to devour." You have got to know that the enemy is not happy about the way God uses you, nor is he excited about many lives that are being drawn to yours. So, what does he do? He lurks and waits. He brings well-meaning individuals in your life under the cover of support and friendship, and he waits. What is he waiting for? The right moment. The moment where your guards are down, and you are vulnerable.

Guarding your mind has a lot to do with not allowing distractions to overtake you. Believe it or not, people can be major distractions to your purpose. If you become so inundated with them, you are probably not being attentive to yourself. The consequence of this is that you are not aware of the things that might be entering in your life as weapons against your progress.

Have you ever seen a magnet, like the ones on the refrigerator, lose its connection? It doesn't sometimes fall all the way off, but it does sometimes slide around. Possibly, it's being used to hold a piece of paper or something, and it's not the magnet that is losing strength, it's the thing in between it and the surface its on. This is what happens when we allow things to come between our relationship with God. It is he that is the watchman of our souls. Whenever you lose touch with him, you lose touch of the light that shines in dark places. This is the best environment for the enemy to do his work, in the darkness.

Here's another lesson that we can pull out of the example of the sliding magnet. It doesn't stay in position. It doesn't stay grounded. Our gifts, anointings, and talents work best when it is grounded and stable. You should live your life based on certain principles that keep you rooted in your values and in what the Lord has called you to do.

"Guard the treasure that was committed to you through the Holy Spirit who lives in us"
2 Timothy 1:14

THE DANGERS OF COMPARING AND COMPETING

If the truth is told, many leaders approach ministry like a sporting event. We not only size each other up, but we offer our best players against those of another ministry to see who can preach the best, raise the greatest offerings and who can grow their churches the fastest. But, Jesus never talked about competition. For him, there was no competition. He knew what he was called to do and went about do that. He was secure in his purpose. For many leaders, their insecurity blinds the biblical demand for unity. God, in his word, speaks clearly against divisions within the body. Countless scriptures promote unity and oneness, and none teach us to compete with one another or to compare ourselves with any other image other than the image of Christ. There's a big difference between gleaning and cloning. You can pull from the example of others without reproducing the exact image of someone else.

One of the dangers of comparing yourself to others is that you lose sight of who you were called to be. If this happens, you'll search for another image that you think is successful and you'll begin to conform to that instead of the authentic purpose that you've been called to master.

Whenever comparison occurs you begin to value what is resident in another instead of being happy about what God has given you. You lose sight of your magnet. It's the thing that God has used to draw others to you. You stop doing what you did to make people come in the first place.

Don't develop the compulsion to compete. You don't have to try to do what you aren't gifted to do. Stay in your lane!

Many churches have seen a great decline, not because God left them, or the vision isn't clear. It's because God gave them a plan, but they wanted to be popular and do it like everyone else. What works for one, doesn't always work for all. You have got to be secure in the methods that God has given you to remain effective in life and ministry. Yes, some things aren't popular, but they are effective? Are souls being won to Christ? Are lives being changed? If the answers to these questions are yes, what more do you want? I've got the answer to that. You want the applause, the validation of your colleagues or those who have gone before you. Here's the sobering part, what you're looking for might never come. You have got to be so solid in what you've been called to do that it doesn't even matter anymore. Your satisfaction comes from a greater place. It comes from the God within.

As we conclude, I want to challenge you to rest and be secure in your role in the plan of God on the earth. Whatever it is that God has given you is worth being protected. Don't ever make the mistake of trying to be anything or anyone that you aren't. This will put you in a very dangerous place and one that many never leave.

There's not a person alive that can compete with you. You are a designer original. You have a magnet and through this God will bring many people to himself through the tremendous gift you continue to be. Stay focused.

ABOUT THE AUTHOR

Daniel Latimer is a leader, Life Coach, Author and Motivational Speaker. He is a husband to LaChish Latimer and a father to five beautiful children. He and family reside in Augusta, Georgia

Made in the USA
Columbia, SC
24 October 2023

24774096R00050